MW00975882

FOR SUCH A TIME AS THIS

FOR SUCH A TIME AS THIS

Hannah L. Drake

Copyright © 2015 by Hannah L. Drake
All rights reserved. This book or any portion thereof may not be
reproduced or used in any manner whatsoever without the express
written permission of the author except for the use of brief
quotations in a book review or scholarly journal.
Scripture quotations are taken from the Holy Bible, King James
Version, Cambridge, 1769. (Public Domain)
Sojourner Truth, Ain't I A Woman
First Printing: 2015
ISBN-13: 978-1512265941
ISBN-10: 1512265942 Hannah L. Drake
www.hannahldrake.com
hld@hannahldrake.com

Hannah C. Drake

DEDICATION

To anyone in the fight for equality and justice for all people, and to my niece, Cleanna Thomas, because perhaps one day when you are older, this will all seem like a dream and humanity will have found equilibrium. Until then, I write.

ACKNOWLEDGEMENTS

Many are called but few, few are chosen
I Have Been Chosen
Plucked from obscurity
To speak a word of life to a dying nation
Oblivious to the fact that circumstances of my life,
of your life, of this world filled with joy and sorrow,
smiles and tears, pain, suffering and triumph
Would provide the manuscript
I made a vow
To speak the Truth
Uncompromised, Unfiltered
Straight with No Chaser
Even if it meant others would know my story
Even if it meant I would be scorned
Even if it meant I would lose friends
Even if it meant the nights would be long and lonely
My mission…set on ancient scrolls
My destiny… written in the heavens
My purpose…determined before birth
My tests-difficult
My life-a series of mountaintops and valleys
My journey-not yet complete
Every day, I write
Hoping that those who read my words will know the
truth
And allow the truth to set them free.

~Keep Reading and I'll Keep Writing~
Hannah Drake

THANK YOU

Thank you to my family, My Mom, Mary Reszel, who always tells me to live in the moment and her husband Paul for always supporting me. My sister, Clevetta, who once told me, "write something else", so I did. Thank you! My niece, Cleanna, who I pray sees a better day, my brother, Chris, a rebel in his own right and to my daughter, my support and my number one fan, Brianna Wright, who is unapologetically black and unapologetically a woman. Embrace them both because for us they go hand in hand. I love you always because you are always who you are with no exceptions!

Thank you to Ferenczy for always supporting and encouraging me to make the best decisions for me-something I have struggled with my entire life. Now is my time.

Thank you to Pastor Williams, who speaks boldly and with no apologies. Continue to do God's work and continue to fight for justice. One does not exist without the other. Thank you to my Bates Memorial Family who always supports me. From day one, I could have written the ABC's and you were in my corner! We are changed people, changing the world, one person at a time! And that is what it is going to take.

Thank you to my poetry family, near and afar, that support my work, encourage me to write and challenge me to continue to grow in my craft.

This collection of poetry was one that was not expected. I had not picked up my pen in months, perhaps years. It was birthed because of injustice, too many lives taken, too many R.I.P. shirts, too many mothers weeping, too many hashtags. For every individual that has become a hashtag, a face on a t-shirt, a social media topic of debate, I pause, and say that I hear you and I pray that I have allowed my words to be your voice. We hear you. Your fight, your death, your cause was not in vain.

Hannah L. Drake

And So It Begins...

IT AIN'T PRETTY

It ain't always pretty cause pretty poetry ain't what we
do
True, roses are red and violets are blue
Even Dr. Seuss can convince you
Thing One and Thing Two can seduce you
Make you deduce that life is a series of fairy tales
And everything is summed up with happy endings
As a poet I would be pretending if I subscribed to this
lie
See this is not the reason that I write
This is not the reason I stay up at night
Puffing on spent buds of nicotine
To give you and your consciousness some smoke
screen
It ain't always pretty…
But no one said it would be
We flow in the underbelly
In the alley
In those dark corners
We are the voices for those walls that can't talk
We are the souls of black bodies lined in chalk
Of those stories you wanna keep hidden
Like why Uncle Jim can't be left with the children
Why Momma has race tracks up and down her veins
Society conceives chaos, poets endure labor pains
And we birth hurt
We birth misery
We birth stories of a round cheek 10 year old girl on
her knees
We birth a banging body infected with HIV
We birth a young boy still stuck in the closet

We birth razor blades with drops of blood that held
promise
We tell the stories that no one else wants to tell
Notebooks singed with the fire of writing through hell
This…is not…PRETTY!
This is that oxymoronic poetry
A beautiful struggle
This is pretty and ugly all wrapped into verse
Even when it feels good at the same time it hurts
This is life
This is struggle
This is pain
This is journals, open Bibles and empty bottles
This is literary sinners seeking poetic salvation
This is the voice of a neglected generation
This is tears shed in a lonely bedroom
This is drunken prayers knelling at a porcelain god
This is Botox illusions giving up the façade
This is that after midnight, high heels in hands, hoe
stroll poetry
This is THE REAL, THE RAW, that you're afraid to
see
With no filter, no bleach, no pre-poetic speech
If you don't WANT IT REAL AND RAW DON'T
ASK ME TO SPEAK!
Cause I know no other way then to give you what's
real
Every time I spill my ink on these pages
It's summing up heartache in poetic phrases
This is not just poetry
These are our stories, our testimonies
Wrapped in nouns, verbs, pronouns, adjectives

Blanketed in literary devices
These words are addicts surrendering vices
This is me…staring at pages…blank pages
Asking God, "What do you want me to say?"
And I listen
Because this is not my voice
The things that I spit ain't my choice
This is not my pen
This is not my paper
So I stare…And the pages stare back at me
Waiting
For the story to be told
I don't just give you poetry I give you pieces of my
soul
Something has left me
For me to give to you, I have to sacrifice me
My ink is on a tightrope
Straddling a fine line of sanity, madness and
depression
Don't get the impression that this is easy because we
make it look easy
And it ain't always pretty
It ain't always Mac foundation and celebrity lip gloss
This costs
It's mutilated muffles
Deformed destinies
Hunchbacked haikus
Dreams deferred
It is life
Tattered
Bruised
Enraptured

Beat down
Loved
Stomped on
Abused
This is poetry
This is David's psalms
Africa's drumbeat
Eric Garner's last words
This is Nina Simone's blackbird
Paul Dunbar's mask
Maya's knowledge of why the caged bird sings at last
This is Rapper's Delight's bang bang boogie
Nas's one mic
Lauryn's Zion
Robert Frost's road not taken
This is Langston's raisin in the sun
Marvin's let's get it on
And when it's all done
This is poetry
Two sides of the same coin
Ugly and Beautiful
Sunshine and Rain
Joy and Pain
Happiness and Sadness
All encompassing
Of the struggle
What a beautiful struggle… poetry…

UNJUST WINDS...

Billows of
Unjust winds wrap around me. Tears...
Rain down, flooding my soul
Nothing is as it seems. As I long for it to be.
Thirst for
Hope
Invades my space. I drink cups of drought and
Sorrow as
Brothers and Sisters face
Injustice.
Tomorrow they say will be a new day...
Clichés of optimism
Hide the
Depths of reality. This reality. Our reality.
Oppression is a
Weight too heavy for me to carry.
Now is the time for revolution.

Hannah L. Drake

THIS IS FOR THE MISFITS

This is for the misfits
The Rabble-rousers
The Not Good Enough's and the You Remind Me of
Your Daddy's
This is for the Rebels
The ones who never had a certain table to sit at in the
lunchroom
The ones that played alone on schoolyard
playgrounds and were always picked last for
dodgeball
That never quite fit into jock or Goth or those drama
kids
That always seemed like a square peg in a round
world
This is for the ones that challenge authority
That don't just take your answer because you say that
is the only answer
This is for the ones that ask why and then why not
That live their life on the precipice of a hypothesis
This is for the variables that refuse to remain constant
This is for the freedom fighters
The Revolutionaries
The By Any Means Necessary's
This is for those on the front line with 99 cent
handkerchiefs masquerading as gas masks
This is for the ones that bellow no justice no peace
That stare in the face of oppression and dare to defy
the system
This is for the other
The Misunderstood

This is for the black girl who was told her skin was too dark to ever be beautiful
For the boy that hangs his sexuality among Gap jeans and polo shirts in closets
For the woman that regurgitates pieces of her self-esteem in plastic bags just so she can look like those on magazine covers
For the man that plays musical beds because he was told that manhood was equated to notches on bedpost
This is for the woman that auctions pieces of her soul each night to the highest bidder
This is for the dropout, the drunk, the addict
The ones who were told you will never amount to anything and yet here they stand
This is for the ones that life counted out because they were never counted in
This is for the agitator, whose very existence makes the status quo uncomfortable
This is for the Hell Raiser
The Nuisance
The Trouble Maker
The Oddball
The Freak
The Anomaly
The Peculiar people
The Visionaries
This is for those
The people that dare to dream that things can be different not one day but now
Because those are the ones that turn the world upside down!

So Be It

If I must fight
If blood must be shed
If I must die
So be it.
"For our struggle is not against flesh and blood,
but against the rulers,
against the powers,
against the world forces of this darkness,
against the spiritual forces of wickedness in the heavenly places."

I refuse to die without a fight
I refuse to remain silent and do nothing
I refuse to regurgitate information with no action
I refuse to accept the status quo
It is with the spirit of Esther, I am courageous
"And if I perish, I perish."
With the bravery of four lepers, I act
"Why do we sit here until we die?"

With the knowledge of my Savior I stand boldly
"No one takes my life away from Me, but I lay it down
on My own initiative. I have authority to lay it down,
and I have authority to take it up again."
With courage, I know that sometimes I must fight
"And from the days of John the Baptist until now the
kingdom of heaven suffereth violence, and the violent
take it by force."

If I must fight
If blood must be shed
If I must die
So be it.
But I refuse to die without trying my damndest
To live with freedom.

(Quoted text is from: Ephesians 6:12, Esther 4:14
2 King 7:3, John 10:18, Mathew 11:12).

BLACK HISTORY R.I.P.

So being Black is popular
The in thing
I wonder when the ending comes
When the fad fades
When the progress of popularity expires
When rap jingles can no longer sale Mickey D's and
Gap attire
When white suburban kids decide
That it is time
to stop kneelin' to their white hip hop God Eminem
And decide to discard their 5th Avenue store bought
Timbs
No longer dappin' with their black friend
on the block 'cause now he has to call you Sir...
When they no longer have a need rock our wear
And now adorn business suits, ties and wing tips
'cause mommy and daddy won't pay for college
unless they get a grip
And set all that so called "Black" stuff aside
Will our culture die?

Will there be a Black culture cemetery littered with
Black artifacts
Like Air Force One's and Lakers throwbacks
Discarded platinum chains, grills, rusty 22's and
pimp chalices
All because we forgot about the calluses
On the hands of those
That labored and toiled
Only for us to pimp our culture to the mainstream

No longer the enemy 'cause we on his team
Fuck a dream when all we care about is that cream
So they lace our pockets with seed money
And we tap dance for them now, so who is the
dummy?
Never knowin' the joke was on us

Because we're foolish enough to trust a system
Whose very existence resides in pimpin'
The weak and the less fortunate
Black is in today, tomorrow they'll say, there it went

Our history buried in a Black cemetery
Cause we pimped out the cross
And we leave it to Timmy and Billy to floss
Until they decide to toss our culture aside
Where all the other "Negro" artifacts reside
Among the other Black debris
Cause we foolishly chromed out our Black History
And the diamond encrusted headstone reads
Black Culture -Forever Rest In Peace

10 & 2

When my daughter turned 17 I decided it was time that we had "the talk".
Only this was a little deeper than the birds and the bees
How do you sit your child down and tell them their reality is not everyone's reality?
That in this world, at times, their ice will seem colder than her ice.

She walked into the house eyes bright and smiling
17 just a few months shy of adulthood
17 just a few months shy of being a woman
17 just a few months shy of leaving my home
17 almost grown yet I felt the need to explain to her
As she skipped in the house flashing her drivers permit
Just how deep this rabbit hole goes
Only she was not Alice and this was not Wonderland
This was not some psychedelic dream

While most parents can celebrate their child receiving their drivers permit
And send them to the store on their first trip for non-essential items like milk and bread
I had to remind her that a holding her hands in the air in an act of surrendering could lead to her with a bullet in her head
I had to remind her that a trip to the store for Skittles and tea could be her death sentence

That playing her music too loudly could lead to me
picking out caskets
While her other high school friends celebrated their
driving permits
I had to explain to her
That driving while black could be criminalistic
That walking will black could be deadly
That breathing while black some have found to be
lethal
That running while black can be costly
That wearing a hoodie could have life or death
consequences
That being black in this world meant staying on
guard...being smart

I sat my child down and said
When, not if, but when, the police pull you over this
is what you do
You keep your hands on the wheel at 10 and 2
And whatever you do, do not make any sudden moves
This is not Law and Order
The police do not shoot to wound
They are shooting to kill you
When they come to your window be polite
It was almost like I was giving her a mandate to shuck
and jive
But in this world I am trying to save her life
Say, "Yes Sir" or "No Sir" and whatever you do, do
not resist
If you give them any reason to kill you this will be
their defense
And being black will be your only offense

Contrary to popular belief, for you, Officer Friendly does not exist
They will simply kill you not for who you are but for what you represent

Do not offer any hesitation
Be prepared when they ask for your license and registration
When they tell you, "Hands on your head," simply assume the formation
And I know even though you are innocent and have no obligation

I do not want see your face on a T shirt
I do not want your last words to be the next profitable slogan
I do not want the validity of your life picked apart by Facebook and Instagram pics
I do not want who you are as a person reduced to the life that could have been
I do not want your story to be a quick sound bite on CNN
I do not want to be one of those mothers' weeping in agony in the streets as their child's blood runs down a drain
And in less than 6 months it will be another name, another face and you…you will be a memory hidden underneath preachers looking for 15 minutes of fame, phony indictments, corruption and a justice system that has turned to a blind eye to righteousness

So this is my message to you, this is the talk
And I know that this is difficult
Every day we swallow down the bitterness of this reality until we feel like we can choke
And when it's time for the revolution you and I will be the first ones to revolt
But right now…right now you are simply a teenage girl that wants to drive
And right now…right now I'm just a mother who wants to save your life
10 & 2

Compared to White drivers, Black drivers are…
✓ 31% more likely to be pulled over
✓ 81% more likely to not be given a reason for it
✓ 174% more likely to be searched
Source: Bureau of Justice Statistics

DYING DECLARATIONS

The weight of a person's last words
Are often too heavy for many to bear
So powerful are a person's last words
The court of law has deemed them a dying
declaration
Suspended hearsay and will admit a person's last
words into evidence…
"Mom, I'm going to college." Amadou Diallo
"I don't have a gun. Stop shooting!" Mike Brown
"What are you following me for?" Trayvon Martin
"I love you, too." Sean Bell
"Why did you shoot me?" Kendrec McDade
"You shot me." Oscar Grant
"Please don't let me die." Kimani Gray
"It's not real." John Crawford
"You promised you wouldn't hurt me!" Natasha
McKenna
"How did switching lanes with no signal turn into all
of this, I don't even know." Sandra Bland
"I can't breathe." Eric Garner
Last words from countless victims
Caught
Suspended
Frozen
Encapsulated in a moment in time
Sealed
Entombed with gunshots, blood and deadly wounds
All because they were
Driving While Black
Biking While Black
Walking While Black

Shopping While Black
Running While Black
Breathing While Black
Just
Existing… While… Black...

ANOTHER BITCH

I want nothing real from you
And
You want nothing real from me
We met on the corner of simplicity
In a downtown motel
Boasting rooms rented by the hour
It was my legs that caught your eye
Toned from endless hours of walking up and down
the boulevard
The legs of a dancer
That long to study at Julliard
Classical ballet
Yet I learned in NYC
More money would be made on my knees
Than dancing on my toes
Who knows if that is true?
All I know is that right now
I discard thoughts of dancing on Broadway
While I dance for you
To misogynistic tunes
That reinforce
My sad belief
That the day I was born
The other unwanted pups in the kennel
Made room
For another bitch...

TRICK, BITCH, HOE

I wonder… when did I became a
Trick
Bitch
Or Hoe
Can someone please tell me
Because I want to know
When my
Black, pecan tan, mahogany
Here before time was time
Labeled once as godly and divine
Set it all into motion when humanity begun
Frenched kissed by the sun
Skin
Became equated with 3 deadly sins
Trick
Bitch
And Hoe
Please let me know
When being a black female became equal to the
richness between my thighs
Please let me know whose feeding you those lies
And why my daughter cries at night
Cause her daddy called her momma a stank ass bitch
The media says she ain't nothin but a trick
And why rappers say she's a damn good hoe if she
shakes it like this
Please let me know
How did I morph from birthing a nation
To a trick bitch and hoe?
And please inform me
When I was dethroned and lost my royalty

And became nothing but a commodity?
An image on the auction block simply to be sold
Just another trick bitch or hoe
Not a woman that has a soul and goals
And even if I do work late at night swinging from a
pole
I'm trying to feed my three kids not a tip tricking,
dick sucking hoe
So today I say fuck your labels
Fuck your "black women were born to breed" fables
Fuck your game-keeping women like they housed in
stables
I am more than able
And capable to know
That here stands a queen, a diva, the epitome of
excellence
Not
A
Trick
Bitch
Or
Hoe!

BACKPACKS & BURDENS

She carries burdens like overweighed book laden
backpacks on scrawny kids with buckling knees
Her frilly Fredrick's of Hollywood French lace
panties hold secrets tightly like Victoria
Pale pink endless thread count Egyptian cotton sheets
now stained with mourning magenta remind her that
nightmares and fairy tales like Janus often wear the
same mask of duality
Life, friendships, dates can turn on a dime
Pals can mutate to predators
Good can morph into evil over steak and lobster
dinners, over cheap burgers and heavily salted French
fries
In a split second when the desire for power meets
vulnerability,
Meets innocence,
Meets a drunken night among "friends"
Shit…just…got…real…

Walls that long to scream from having seen too much
remain silent
Shouts become whispers in shadows
Cries resolve to simply whimpering in cramped, dusty
corners
Muffles are muted against pillowcases that encase
no's and stop's and why's

A night of drinks now turned into a lifetime of her
drowning in sorrow
It was simply a night out on the town with friends
It was simply dinner

It was simply coming over for pizza
It was simply a walk to the park
It was simply…simply…simply existing
It was simply vodka on ice in rock glasses
Beer in freezer chilled mugs
Wine in gold rimmed glasses
Champagne in crystal flutes
Rape has no class
From milk bottles to shaken not stirred martini glasses
We, as women, enter the world always reaching, clawing, begging
Always in an act of surviving
We burn bras
We march too
We wear miniskirts that defy gravity
We bare, bare chests in deviance
Claiming that we are taking back the night
Retrieving what was stolen from us
We keep attempting to take it back
Because we have never regained it
The night continues to be stolen
Robbing our days
Taking our afternoons hostage

24 hours a day we stand on guard
From back alleys to bedrooms to boardrooms
None of us are immune
Because we…we are women
Like diamond mines in Africa I wish my words were deeper, richer
However the fact is that the day we were born the Universe birthed tears of joy and streams of sorrow

Because it knew the heartache that we would endure
Society is obsessed with the breaking of beauty
Tantalized by torture
Seduced by grown women in school girl skirts and
Mary Jane shoes
Men seeking to fulfill childhood fantasies of fucking
cheerleaders behind worn bleachers

She never knew nor had a clue that a night out for
drinks, a night hanging with the guys would end up
like this...
The statement of her no now interpreted through the
lenses of her clothing, her shoes, the way she wears
her hair, her perfume, how many men she has slept
with, that she would be deemed a whore yet her
masculine counterparts applauded for their vitality...
Here she would not be equal...
Who knew that two letters – N & O could be endlessly
debated in courtrooms?

Fault would be laid at the doorstep of her womanhood
Condemnation now wrapped up in her robust
sexuality
Verdicts of not guilty often speak too loudly rendering
victims silent
So she swallows the blame and eats bad choices
Regurgitating the details of nights that haunt her with
hypothetical theories of if and then and what and why

"I should have" and "If I could do it all over again"
has now become the theme song of her life
As she spends nights with tears chain linked to cheeks

Wondering if the pieces that he stole from her will ever be given back to her again on a day that she is least expecting happiness to return to her like misaddressed packages?

On those nights, childhood night lights keep away bogeymen and monsters that conceal themselves in corner deepness
Just once she longs to be that woman again
That woman with her guard down
That didn't flinch at sounds
That did fear shadows lurking in corners
That covered her drinks at parties with non-kryptonite white paper napkins
That wore miniskirts and stilettoes
That twirled on daiquiri stained dance floors
That didn't wonder about the motives of every man that she met
That slept…peacefully and when she slept she dreamed vivid dreams that were not on instant replay of that night that her life was altered, her peace stolen…

Just once she longs to be whole again
So she spends days attempting to pick up the fragments of a life irrevocably shattered
Trying to forget
Yet always finding herself remembering
The weight of him, the stench of him, the bitterness, and the pain of a life forever changed from one night that was supposed to be like any other night
Only this time life had other plans

Yet somewhere deep inside she resolves to gather those pieces,
Fighting to grasp at them yet feeling like she is clutching at vapors
Similar to picking up fistfuls of sands,
Holding her fingers tightly vowing never to allow one piece of herself to escape again…

TODAY IS THE DAY

Power
The capacity or ability to influence the behavior of others or the course of events
Power
Physical might
Power
The energy or motive force by which a physical system or machine is operated
Power
That thing that is placed inside of you
Rumbling deep in your gut
Flowing in your veins
Making your heart beat
That feminine instinct
That allows an ordinary woman to do extraordinary things
That allows a high school drop out to go back to school
That allows a woman beat down to leave an abusive relationship
That gives a woman the strength to say, "I love you but I love myself a little bit more."
That thing that says not tomorrow
Not when I retire
Not when I turn 40
Not at the start of the New Year
But TODAY

Today is the day
That I will muster up the power within in me to take
back everything that was stolen from me
To fulfill my dreams
To walk away from a job that doesn't pay me what I
am worth
To look cancer in the face and say give me your best
shot
Today is the day
That I declare diabetes doesn't have to be
generational
That the curse of molestation ceases with me
To stop living paycheck to paycheck
That I become a role model to my children
That I recognize if I'm good enough to sleep with
than I am good enough to marry

Today is the day
That the pity party comes to an end
That the time for excuses is over
Today is the day that I declare
I will no longer live defeated
I will not dim my light in order for you to feel
brighter
I was born to shine
I am more than a conqueror
I can do all things through Christ that strengthens me
I am a righteous woman that falls down seven times
but gets up eight
I am fearfully and wonderfully made

I am a woman
With unlimited possibilities and infinite potential
I possess the power
To make daydreams reality
To make my life one that matters
Today is the day
That I walk into my destiny
I can be whatever I desire to be
I am whoever I say I am
And today…today I say I am
Strong, Beautiful, Wise, Determined, Intelligent
Gorgeous, Revolutionary, Authentic, Destined for
Greatness

I am a woman that loves hard and strong
I am a woman that loves pink frilly things
And who struts in stilettos and embraces her curves
unapologetically
I am a woman that revels in being a woman
Being treated like a lady
But never attempt to paint me in a corner
Because baby was NEVER meant to be in a corner
My life cannot be defined by coloring in lines
I am 3 hundred and 60 degrees of pure femininity
Bolstered by His promises to me

And today is the day that we access our power
And by doing that
We give permission for another woman to grasp hers
To shine, to grow, to illuminate all that God has
placed inside of her

Someone right now, right this very moment, is
waiting on you to be all that you can be
So that they can be all they are destined to be
We are the key to someone's lock
We are the epitome of power
We are strength personified
And together we have the power to change
communities, to change policies, to change lives,
And to finally exhale
Deeply…and just breathe… with ease
Today is the day
We possess our power!

HAVE YOU EVER HEARD A SOUL SCREAM?

When the pain is too much
When the desire for what you want is that profound
When the hurt wraps around arteries and vessels and rips
through veins
When your heart actually feels severed in your chest
When the thought of going on is almost unbearable
When everything around you is telling you to quit
When you know that type of pain
Where the core of who you are is aching
When your soul is screaming
That is when you call on him
From the depths of your innermost being
Jesus help me!
Keep me!
Hold me up!
Have you ever heard a soul scream?
A sound so loud
That it resonates in the Heavens
And in that moment
Everything you have ever wanted to say is expressed in
that scream
Every desire
Every wish
Everything you have ever longed for
Everything you have ever lost
Today I scream for those silenced
For those who voices were stolen
I scream for justice, liberty, equality, love and freedom
I scream for mothers that mourn and women that wail
I scream for men that were told that men do not shed tears
Scream boldly and believe that there is hope in your
hollering
Let it out and know that he hears you…

RIGHTEOUS BLACK SISTA

I tried to break through the glass ceiling
But I still got 80 cents to the man's dollar anyway

I tried to stay in the house and build a home
But you still had an affair anyway

I tried to dress in 9 West pumps and corporate suits
But you undressed me with your eyes anyways

I tried to achieve a dream
But you called me a nappy headed hoe anyway.

I tried to encourage my child to be creative
But you labeled him as having Attention Deficit
Disorder anyway

I tried to set an example by labeling myself a
QUEEN
But you labeled me a bitch anyway

I tried to uplift my sisters with words
But you called me a revolutionary dyke anyway

I tried to live my life above the standard
But you gossiped about me anyway

I tried doing it your way
And trying, as they say, is still failing
Just failing with honor
So today...I take a stand

No more trying
Today I am doing!
I am doing it my way
And my way
Is saying
Fuck the status quo
I am a righteous black sista!!

AIN'T I A WOMAN 2015

In 1851 Sojourner Truth proudly stood at a Women's
Convention in Akron, Ohio and declared 4 words
that 164 years later still ring true
Ain't I A Woman?
Seeing the femininity of my God given curves
Seeing the 360 degrees of my womanhood
The roundness of my hips
The fullness of my lips
Many would deem this question to be one of a
rhetorical nature
And as I stand before you today all that I can say is
the same thing that she declared back in 1851
Ain't I A Woman?
I know that I often times we make this look easy
Balancing the weight of the world on my shoulders
while rocking 4 inch stilettoes
Making sure my Mac makeup is flawless to the
untrained eye it seems simple
But baby ain't I a woman?
Sometimes it is easier to wear high heels and conceal
the pain that is seeping in your veins
Because you…you were simply in the shower letting
Calgon take you away when you discovered the lump
in your breast that plagues 1 in every 8 women
You were doing nothing but being you…when they
discovered you had cervical cancer
You were simply being a woman on the career path
when you discovered age and ambition had robbed
you of motherhood
But Ain't I A Woman
Women want nothing different than you do

Respect has no gender
Money should hold the same value for the same work
Yet when I walk into the boardroom I know that is not
my degrees but my D's that will garner your attention
If I demand respect I will not be seen as a woman on
the fast track to CEO
I will be that woman with an attitude…the ice queen
When did demanding respect become synonymous
with being a problem?
Only in this world can a woman be on the verge of
becoming the leader of the nation
And we do not blog or ask questions about her
policies, her thoughts on international relations, her
programs to deal with unemployment
Yet we will ask what designer is she wearing?
Why does she wear her hair like that?
Whose shoes does she have on?
Because of course, when it comes to women, that is
what society deems as important.
Yet Aint I A Woman?
Only for me can the decision to give birth be debated
and decided in courtrooms
And judges that sit on benches decide what I will do
with my womb
Anything that I want to do with my body is up for
debate
And the stake of my fate is now held in the hands of
men
That will never give birth
Who do not understand the trials of being a single
mother with 3 kids that you are already struggling to
provide for…

That will never understand looking through a magazine that deems you as unworthy because you do not fit into a supermodel mold

Who have never been overwhelmed with images that you know you will NEVER look like

Men that will never understand choking down the pain of being molested because your mother looked the other way because he paid the bills

The agony you carry because you know although you said no your mini skirt to society said yes

The sadness in your eyes when your daughter longs to be a doctor but every toy in the aisle encourages her to dream no higher than to scramble eggs and vacuum floors

Yet, AINT I A WOMAN

You cannot put me in my place

Baby was never meant to be in a corner

As Sojourner Truth said so well,

"That man over there say a woman needs to be helped into carriages and lifted over ditches and to have the best place everywhere.

Nobody ever helped me into carriages or over mud puddles or gives me a best place. . .

And ain't I a woman?

Look at me! Look at my arm! I have plowed and planted and gathered into barns and no man could head me. . .

And ain't I a woman?

I could work as much and eat as much as a man- when I could get to it-and bear the lash as well

And ain't I a woman?

I have born 13 children and seen most all sold into slavery and when I cried out a mother's grief none but Jesus heard me. . .
And ain't I a woman?
That little man in black there say a woman can't have as much rights as a man cause Christ wasn't a woman. Where did your Christ come from? From God and a woman!
Man had nothing to do with him!
If the first woman God ever made was strong enough to turn the world upside down, all alone together women ought to be able to turn it right-side up again!"
So in 2015 I still declare AINT I A WOMAN!

JUST LISTEN TO ME

If you want to reach me...
Just listen to me. Hear Me. Understand me
See life through my wide brown eyes....
See here the sun don't shine
Cause it's always dripped in crimson shades of blood
I have watched 3 of my homeboys gunned downed
just for walkin in the wrong hood
Lil Tony still has bullet fragments in his back. He
shows them proudly.
I have been to 10 funerals in the last 2 years -thought
the young weren't supposed to die
But bullets have no eyes and Tina was only 8, killed
in a drive by
as she double-dutched outside.
I lie awake while helicopters fly overhead,
Heart beating in my chest as I wonder just once will
I ever sleep with peace
I weep tears as I watch another "uncle" come into
my house
And I hurt because I know this uncle will soon
violate the only thing that I know that makes me a
man.
I am confused trying to be both a child and a
grownup-
Cause somebody's got to be the man of this house.
And it sure won't be my momma,
cause she's off on her own thing
Another face, another name, just as long as they drop
a little change this will never change
I watch homicides on TV..."in today's news another
black male dead"...and I flip the channel

to rappers in Bentleys, poppin' Cris and telling me a
woman ain't nothin' but a bitch
And hey that's what the pimp says, when he lies in
my momma's bed and she gives him head
And I...and I.....and I cry those project tears that can
only be shed in dark rooms
As darkness consumes my soul
I am reaching, searching, longing
for direction but no one will LISTEN TO ME
You want to know how to help me?
Do not overlook my story
Recognize that times are different
I see kids hop-scotching over crack vials and dirty
needles
I see Trojan wrappers lying in the middle of the
street
Instead of kicking rocks I kick spent bullets on my
way to school
I am at war and these images are the shrapnel
piercing my soul.
My daddy's doing a 20 year bid upstate
And still says he's gonna buy me that bike ONCE
HE GETS OUT
but my friends are PUSHING WHIPS
And wearing Jordan's and rocking designer fits
Bought with drug money and all I need is a little bit
Maybe I can do something to get my momma
out of this roach infested hell where she pimps her
kids
to keep the lights on
And my brother is a crack baby screaming for a fix
that Similac can't itch.

And my sister has AIDS yet can't afford her medicine
So she treats her tricks for hits to make the pain go away.
I am not living
I AM MERELY SURIVING
Surviving like an animal in this jungle
Like back in the day they would say
DON'T PUSH ME CAUSE I'M CLOSE TO THE EDGE
I'M TRYIN NOT TO LOSE MY HEAD
Now all I know is to GET RICH OR DIE TRYING
And I think maybe just maybe that is what I need to do.
DIE TRYING
Because I'm dying anyway.
From the cradle to grave
Maybe <u>then</u> someone will mourn me
Maybe <u>then</u> someone will listen to me
When they see, that I was just another black boy doing time in this game called life
And circumstances had already sentenced me to die
SO HELP ME, LISTEN TO MY CRIES
CAN'T YOU HEAR THEM?!
LISTEN TO MY SILENT SCREAMS IN THE MIDDLE OF THE NIGHT
Overlaid with prayers
Cause one day I think I'm gonna make it Heaven
But right, now, right now I'm living in hell on Earth
AND I NEED HELP!
I AM SCREAMING
YELLING!!

48

PLEADING!!
JUST LISTEN TO ME!!

THEY WILL NEVER KNOW
Dedicated to Brianna and Hannah

They will never know
Because they refuse to see
Because in this world
In this life
In this existence
All things are black and white
No variants
No shades of gray
Just black or white
So they will never take an ounce of time to know my
daughter
Do you know
When she falls down and scrapes her knee it bleeds
red blood
And she is afraid of the dark
And loves ice cream with brownies
And pepperoni pizza
But
They will never know because they refuse to see
That their daughter and my daughter
Both love pink
Day dream of their first kiss
Loved Barbie Dolls
And Disney Channel
Love pom poms and middle school cheers
Long to be the prom queen
But
They will never know
Because they don't want to see
That my daughter

Like their daughter
Day dreams of a future
Longs to be a doctor or school teacher
Desires to be brilliant
They will never know because they refuse to see
That they are more alike than they could ever be
different
They don't teach love and compassion
They don't teach understanding and love
They don't teach equality and peace
Nowadays studies don't extend beyond reading,
writing, and arithmetic
No extracurricular activities on humanity
No tutors for basic instructions for navigating
through this life filled with diversities
They will never know
Because they cannot see
That if they had let our daughters play together
They could have accomplished much together
And at the very least
They could have been friends.

AND THE SAGA CONTINUES

Africa
Motherland
Home
Free
Captured
Bound
Chains
Confined
Slave Ship Sardines
Stripped
Beaten
Sold
Auctioned
Separated
Cotton Fields
Sunrise to Sunset
Negro Spirituals
Swing Low Sweet Chariot coming
forth to carry me home
Tell old Pharaoh to let my people
go
House Nigger
Field Nigger
Uncle Tom
Strange Fruit
Harriet Tubman
Escape
Emancipation
Jubilation
Mentally Bound
Physically Free

Hannah L. Drake

W.E.B.
Booker T
Martin Luther King
Malcolm X
Rosa Parks
Fire Hoses
Jim Crow
Separate but Equal
Colored Only
Whites Only
Back of the Bus
Boycott
Struggle
Survival
Overcome
Endure
Resist
I Have a Dream
Free at Last, Free At Last
Pray
Fight
Brown vs. the Board of Education
What do we want? Freedom!
When do want it? NOW!!
Assassinations
Black Panther
Huey Newton
Black Power
Black Fist
Black Love
Black is Beautiful
Fight the Power
Rodney King

Tupac
Biggie
Yes We Can
President Obama
Trayvon Martin
Hands Up Don't Shoot
Mike Brown
Tamir Rice
Rakia Boyd
Eric Garner
I Can't Breathe
Freddie Gray
Oscar Grant
Kimani Gray
Sandra Bland
Charleston, South Carolina
Police Brutality
Black Lives Matter
Commodity
Trapped
Enslaved
Mentally Bound
Invisible Chains
Fighting for justice
STILL Shackled
And the saga continues...

A DREAM REMIXED

On a sweet summer day in 1963, Martin Luther King bravely stood on the steps of the Lincoln Memorial and declared, "But one hundred years later, the Negro still is not free. One hundred years later, the life of the Negro is still sadly crippled by the manacles of segregation and the chains of discrimination. One hundred years later, the Negro lives on a lonely island of poverty in the midst of a vast ocean of material prosperity. One hundred years later, the Negro is still languishing in the corners of American society and finds himself an exile in his own land. So we have come here today to dramatize a shameful condition."

I stand before you today my brothers and my sisters and I declare that the Black Man is still not free. As long as a black bachelor's blood can drain in the gutters of a New York City Street, no we are still not free. As long as racial slurs can spill from the sweeten tongues of society's privileged, no my brothers and sisters we are still not free. As long as the most powerful country in the world continues to turn a blind eye to the rape and pillage of those in the Sudan, no my brothers and my sisters we are still not free. As long as the Supreme Court continues to challenge Brown vs. the Board of Education, no my brothers and my sisters we are still not free. As long as a hurricane can sweep through the streets of New Orleans littered with the bloated bodies of Black women and children and the administration looks in the other direction, no my brothers and sisters we are still not free.

I must stand before you and declare, do not be impressed or overwhelmed with the tokens that this country has reluctantly given us. I stand today and say that these tokens are nothing but guilt-plated trinkets used to blind us from the true challenges that we continue to face. Do not be deceived my brothers and my sisters, although we have overcome many a mountain, we still must continue on this journey of freedom. As my Brother in this crusade Armah declared, "That we the Black people are one people we know. Destroyers would travel long distances in their minds and out to deny you this truth. We do not argue with them, the fools. Let them presume to instruct us about ourselves. That too is in their nature. That too is in the flow of their two thousand seasons against us. I urge you to continue on with this fight for liberation."

Because as Martin had a dream I too have a dream.....

I have a dream the one day Black Entertainment TV will cease showing our beautiful Queens as sexual objects but celebrate their true inner beauty.

I have dream that the projects will no longer be consumed with generations of families but that we will break the curse of poverty.

I have a dream that Black men and Black women will build the foundation of the Black family and choose to raise their children in a solid home.

Yes, I have a dream today!

I have a dream that a Black Coach can win the Superbowl and the spotlight will not be cast on his race but shone on his character.

I have dream that liquors stores will no longer litter the streets of our community.

I have a dream that pharmaceutical companies will have mercy on our brothers and sisters suffering with AIDS.

I have a dream that we will no longer fund senseless wars but fight genocide in Africa.

I have a dream that young Black men will be offered Ivy League scholarships not because they can bounce a ball but because they can read a book.

I have a dream that a Black man be President and be given a fair chance in the heart of this nation.

I have a dream my brothers and my sisters that my Black daughter will no longer be bussed to a quality school to receive a well-rounded education.

I have a dream because I have planted a seed in this world. I may not see it in my time but like Martin, I have been to the mountaintop, and I have looked over the other side. I look and search for our future Malcolm's, and Garvey's and King's. My eyes roam for our future Maya's, Hurston's, Langston's and Giovanni's. I long to find our future Coretta's and Rosa's because I know if God was to call me on to glory, these soldiers in the fight would continue the dream because a dream can never die.

My brothers and my sisters, although one day we will walk the streets of gold do not wait for the great by and by.

For God declared that He came so that we could live and live now!

And when that time of true freedom comes we will all sing in a voice of unified liberation,
Lift every voice and sing, till earth and Heaven ring,
Ring with the harmonies of liberty;
Let our rejoicing rise, high as the listening skies,
Let it resound loud as the rolling sea.
Sing a song full of the faith that the dark past has taught us,
Sing a song full of the hope that the present has brought us;
Facing the rising sun of our new day begun,
Let us march on till victory is won!

DANCING TO THE BEAT

Contrary to what you have been told
There is no war on drugs
There is no war on crime
As they say in the hood let me drop a dime and put
you up on game
Most of the people that I know do not own airplanes
Cannot bring cocaine or heroin into the United States
Yet somehow
You have been sold a lie
And I'm not a surprise
Cause we'll believe a delusion because somehow that
makes it easier for us to sleep at night
Often times it is easier to cuddle up with a lie as long
as we can convince ourselves that it is the truth

Because we believed what we were taught
These clear lines of demarcation
That there are good guys and there are bad guys
That there are cops and there are robbers
That the world is black and white
With no shades of gray
You did the crime you did the time
We believed we existed in a world where the scales of
justice were balanced
And lady justice was fair, impartial, and she was blind
to things like race, class and gender…

But now…now you have the fox guarding the hen
house
Crime is now big business
Please don't miss this

Crime is now seen as profit
If it lines their pockets then why would they stop it?
Somebody's gotta get paid
From the jumpsuits, the sheets even down to the lunch trays
If they can get rich from stepping on your back then that's what they'll do
It's not that everyone falls through the crack,
It's that releasing you depletes their bank account so they want you back

So what they do is make it as difficult as they can
On your application when they ask, "have you ever been arrested," just check the box, I'm sure they'll understand
And then just to add the cherry on top they put you on paper for the next 3 years
And cause they know you can't pay parole you'll be right back up in here
Because you…you are part of a cycle and believe me baby it's vicious
And cause you're naïve to the system sadly you miss this
You sweetheart ain't nothing but a cog in a wheel
When it comes to your life the prison system and government already struck a deal
They build prisons based off of your status in the third grade
Before you learn to multiply the plans have already been made
They ain't in the business of subtraction they're in the business of addition

When you rally for advancement they ain't motivated to listen

So tell me why they would be concerned with schools in your neighborhood being better?

Why should they care that a juvenile record is like a scarlet letter

You ain't nothin' but a product and they're in the business of building a brand

When it comes to the prison system one hand always washes the other

From the top all the way down to the bottom, they got the system covered

So take me out to the ballgame cause they're waiting on your third strike

They got the bases loaded, like Mayweather and Manny they already fixed the fight

And if you got a problem with that ask Ferguson if you'll end up like Mike

Cause you...you never even stood a chance,

From the womb to the tomb they play the beat and you simply dance

You are the puppet and they hold all the strings

Until you recognize the game nothing will ever change

This is nothing new, simply the thread of oppression that has been woven through the very fabric of this nation

And until it affects you, you will simply call injustice, justified incarceration

WHITE GIRL WASTED...

Tonight... tonight we gonna get White Girl Wasted
White Girl Faded
Tonight...tonight we getting White Girl lifted
Mind bendin' and twisted
It don't matter what our gift is
See I'm on scholarship for bouncing a ball
And me, I can toss one in the air against them all
But tonight, tonight I'm willin' to toss all that aside
with no consequence
(Supposedly)
This bitch got a fat ass and it don't make no sense
She hollering hit it, so that's what I'm gonna do
And when I'm done, I heard she a ho, so I toss her to
my crew
Cause tonight, tonight I'm gonna get White Girl
Wasted
Throwing up in toilets and sinks
Tittering on the brink of insanity
Can't you see me...?
Pour out some liquor! Give me a shot of Hennessy!
Cause tonight, tonight we gonna get White Girl
Wasted
Pull out the Grey Goose and Patron
Baby want a Tsunami? She wanna ride my cyclone
Because tonight, tonight we are getting White Girl
Wasted
Then...then...the horizon comes
In the morning...
Amidst the vomit, Trojan wrappers, discarded thongs
Here comes...here comes the handcuffs

Only this is not 50 shades of gray…
This is not a BDSM cinematic escapade
There are no shades of gray and white or anything in between
Funny how everything looks when you are Black….justice almost pales by comparison
You are atoning for an alleged sin, a whistle that adorned the lips of Emmett Till
Innocent until proven guilty no longer fits the bill
Because you…you got White Girl Wasted
Funny, now how bittersweet vanilla versus chocolate tasted
Never realizing that in that moment you were nothing but a big black buck
That could shuck and jive and even fuck better than then rest of them
Inches were endless
And she begged you to go deeper
So you did
Because she was just pussy
And for many men pussy has no face and certainly no color
Until the next day…the next day…when things are painstakingly Black and White
While you are carving notches in your bed post
She is sitting in police stations
Wondering how she went against everything Mommy and Daddy ever taught her
And the shame and guilt from a black man that runs down her thighs, lingers over her like a stench
So now you know the charge
A charge you have been guilty of for years...

Never knew you were America's Most Wanted
because you could bounce or throw a ball.
And they loved you, they revered you, they chanted
your name.
Believe me, Hosanna can turn to crucify him in a
moment.
Yet still you insist on getting White Girl Wasted,
faded
Refusing to believe they have wanted to indict you,
not now, but centuries ago
For sleeping with "their women"
And what you face now is simply retribution in their
eyes

AND NOW FOR THE REST OF THE STORY… ONLY THIS IS HOW THE STORY WOULD HAVE WENT

"Today we celebrate Columbus Day in honor of a man that came to a foreign land and had thanksgiving with the natives already inhabiting a land that he "discovered". Thank goodness for the Nina, Pinta and the Santa Maria!"

"Immigrants invading America seeking betterment for their families need to go back where they came from! This is America. No one gets a free pass."

"Two misunderstood, youthful males stumbled upon their parents licensed AK-47's and preceded to empty said weapons at their school where they had been victimized by classmates. One of the young men has been in counseling for ADHD and is currently on Ritalin."

"Two nig-excuse us, THUGS, allegedly affiliated with gang violence wreak havoc on inner city school with guns found in their father's a.k.a. baby daddy's room. Where is the mother?"

"Young, misguided, teen mother leaves child on the steps of a church on Christmas day having many in the community affectionately call the baby Jesus and wondering if the mother should be called Mary."

"Sixteen year old African American heathen abandons child in treacherous weather conditions on Christmas of all days. Does she have no soul?"

"College frat prank accidentally goes wrong -boys will be boys!"
"Once again another HBCU (whatever that is) and their militant so called brotherhood caught hazing members."

"College town, such as Lexington, erupted in harmless fun in the streets after basketball team wins the coveted NCAA Championship. Fires were set to keep those in the streets warm. How bout that game?!"
"Swarms of degenerate, low-lifes and thugs riot and set city ablaze to protest so called 'injustice'".

"Today at 5- City official's adult child found with marijuana in car and prescription pills -said to be under medical care and we are sure the marijuana was medicinal. You will hear nothing else of this story. Now for the weather?"
"Yet again police arrest male found with very small amount of weed and pills in a bottle. With the 3 strikes and you are out law, this guy is a goner."

"After hurricane sweet, innocent, kindly family forges for food to survive."
"After God sent his wrath on the place of the unholy to rid the city of lowlifes, a family of stragglers looted stores for food. Probably looking for chicken."

"Police apprehend troubled man that had a bomb, sawed off rifle, grenades, and manifesto of why he hates the police. Even after shots were fired at the police, police managed to arrest him without incident."

"Police shoot and kill man in the street allegedly (term used lightly) with his hands up surrendering. Apparently, man morphed into The Hulk and the policeman feared for his life. We all would have done the same thing. Let's have a moment of silence for the police officer who is on paid leave that he enjoys his vacation time and manages to catch of few of those sunny rays! Now for the weather. Take it away, Jim."

"Kids outside playing cops and robber with toy guns. Oh the nostalgia!"

"Officer kills child outside at park, playing with alleged toy gun. Never play with toy guns or this will be the outcome. How dare he!"

"Your friendly neighborhood watch member follows THUG purchasing suspect items-allegedly tea and Skittles and feels threatened after pursuing him. Kills THUG and earns the key to the city."

"Woman fire gun allegedly in…the…air (side eye)…certainly deserves prison time."

"President claims Weapons of Mass Destruction leading us into war, gives big banks the ability to give home loans to the less fortunate-who should have known they couldn't afford the loans and a host of other things and by golly he is the best president of our time."

"President wants Americans to have affordable health care, lowers gas prices, fights for equal wages for women, wants to increase minimum wage-worst President ever. Who needs health care and why should women be paid the same pay for the same amount of work?"

"In today's news we remember the Holocaust. Let us NEVER forget the horrible atrocities set upon a people because they were deemed different."
"Slavery…Sheesh how long ago was that? Get over it."

"9/11. Let's take a moment to remember…"
"Civil Rights? My goodness that was ages ago. I just don't know why we have to keep talking about this."

And now a word from our sponsors….

HIS NAME WAS KENNETH WINFIELD

His name was Kenneth Winfield
A homeless man that died on the steps of a homeless shelter
A million thoughts ran through my mind reading this news
Most importantly I wondered how does a homeless man die on the steps of a homeless shelter
In freezing temperatures?
Irony sometimes is not without its cruelty
I do not know if he was black or white and truly for me that is irrelevant
Down on your luck comes in all shades
Needing a hand up covers the spectrum of colors
Hardship comes in a variety of hues
I do not know if his parents are still alive
if he was married
if he tried his hand at love and lost
I do not know if somewhere in this world he has children
I am not aware of his education, if he had a GED or a PhD
What I do know is that every life has a story
No one starts life with ambitions of saying,
"I want my first home to be underneath a bridge."
"I want to wear designer rags."
"I want to sale my body on the street corner to provide for my children."
"I want to dine from the finest trash cans in the world."
"I want to die on the steps of a homeless shelter."
Old Man Winter gathered a spring in his step this year

And if anytime you want to know what controls the world simply look at Mother Nature
At times Mother Nature can be cruel and she quakes and she shakes until she is satisfied...
However I was always taught that we have four seasons Winter, Spring, Summer and Fall
All are necessary yet we are inconvenienced by winter
Digging out our BMW's from inches of snow
Pulling out our Chanel winter boots
Adorning our bodies in leather gloves lined in fur, gracing our necks with fashionable scarves
Rushing to the store to swipe our credit cards gathering milk, bread and eggs
Returning to our warm homes to watch Netflix...
Winter is not a welcomed season- it is an irritation because it disrupts our fabulous lifestyles
However the seasons are supposed to change
That is what is supposed to happen
However what shouldn't happen is a man should not freeze to death on the steps of a homeless shelter
Shame on us
Shame on us for our better them than me attitude
When many of us are one and if you are lucky two paychecks away
1 illness away
1 car accident away
1 scandal away
1 death of a spouse away
From being homeless
From being a nameless face in a food line, waiting on a warm bed, sleeping underneath a bridge, sleeping

with random men, revolving faces just to have a few
dollars to buy a few things…
Because it is the Kenneth's of the world today and it
is you and me tomorrow
How does a homeless man die on the steps of a
homeless shelter?
It is because to us, he was invisible and we never saw
him anyway…

I AM NOT INVISIBLE

I am not invisible
Should you place your hand on my chest
You would see that
My heart beats in rhythm to the tune of a life robbed
Of what could have been
Blood still races through my veins
Reminding me
That I am alive
I have purpose
Although you may have discarded me
I am not worthless
I…still…exist
As I lay under a starry canvas
Belly growling as it digests should have's and
wishes
Resting my head on pillows of regrets
Blanketing myself in daydreams
I remember
I remember a time when life was not like this
But life can happen to us all
As you walk by me
Sipping your 5 dollar latte
Turning your nose up
To the stench of my reality
Please know that you are not immune
Life is no respecter of person
Life does what it wants
How it wants
When it wants
And we…we simply yield

There was a time
Perhaps moons ago
When titles like doctor or lawyer
Didn't seem foreign to me
I dreamed big
I was gonna be that kid that made it
There was a time
When phrases like stock market crash were unknown
When downsizing didn't mean giving up your home
To reside on the streets
Where you resort to picking leftovers out of luxury
hotel trash cans so your children can eat
Or to selling what was once held in such high value
for cheap
Because somehow, for me, living has turned to
merely surviving
Yet even with all of that, I would be lying
If I did not admit
That some circumstances I have dug with my own
hands
Promises I made to myself that I couldn't keep
Even on the streets addictions rob me of my sleep
And they creep up and steal my days
Please know every single day I pray
Pray for one more chance
Pray to have an opportunity to do it all over again
There is no condemnation you can place on me that I
do not wrap myself in daily
My life was not supposed to be like this
I wanted so much for myself, so much for my kids
Still every day I sit hoping that job applications don't
require addresses or phone numbers

Business suits or high heels
And still…still I believe
That perhaps this day will be different than the next
day
That perhaps one day you will not overlook me
You will not just toss me your lint covered change
But perhaps one day you will stop and ask me my
name
Because I have one
I am human
I am not trash wrapped in flesh
I am your mentally ill
I am your alcoholic
I am your addict
I am your mothers,
Your daughters
I am your fathers
I am your sons
I am that person that you once loved
And perhaps, perhaps you still do
I am the same person who still dreams, dreams and
still hopes for another day
Notice me
See me
Hear me
I exist
I am here
I am not invisible

I WILL NOT APOLOGIZE FOR MY BLACK

I will not apologize for my black so excuse me if the melanin in my skin makes you uncomfortable
I will not apologize for remembering slavery,
that my ancestors were packed in slave ships like sardines
Stolen, bought, sold, beaten and raped,
working from sun up to sun down in fields for your profit and amusement,
that women like me played wet nurse to your kids and still had to call them Sir.
That my people were whipped for noncompliance, strung up in trees for their so called deviance,
I will not apologize for remembering the tragedy of slavery because it makes you uncomfortable
Why do you want me to forget that but ask me to never forget the Holocaust?
You want me to forget because you don't want to remember
It's terrifying to face the truth
It's strange what shakes from the leaves of the family tree when you start digging at the roots
Strange fruit
But just so you know, you are not Tom Sawyer and I am not Huck Finn
You cannot bribe me to white wash my history
No I do not apologize
For hamhocks, collard greens, cornbread and butter beans
It's not my fault that you gave us the scraps and we turned it into a five star meal…

Don't expect me to apologize that you are just now discovering kale
Wanna add kale to everything like you are discovering something new
Well I been picking greens since before I knew how to tie my shoes
I will not apologize for the rise in my backside or the thickness of my thighs, the fullness of my lips and the shashay in my hips
See this can be surgically imitated but true realness is never duplicated
This ain't nothing but God's nature, and good down home cooking,
Don't get mad at me if you caught your man looking
I will not apologize for my slang, my jive, giving me some skin on the black side, fist pumps and finger snaps
I will not apologize for my roller wrap, braids, locs, or my afro
Fried, dyed, laid to the side, won't even apologize for my soul glo
Won't apologize that when I go au natural you feel threatened
As if your unnecessary fear makes me feel less than
No. It doesn't because I am in touch with who I am
I won't apologize for loving black love and loving a black man
Because I understand that the image you portray is not the one that I know
See I know Black men that would give up everything, even down to their very soul

To support their family, to strengthen their kids, to provide a stable home

You want to paint the image that every black man is gone and if not they are sitting in jail

You write this fairy tale because you have laid out the system, but everyone is not fooled

See now I can tell you, I clearly see the emperor has no clothes

And you want me to apologize as if I have been snowed?

I will not make any apologies for my blackness

And it comes in many shades, various degrees of black

And there is no good black or bad black,

See I would not have passed a brown bag test

But that doesn't make me any more or my caramel sistas any less

From deep, dark black to vanilla black

Black it is simply black and always will be black

And I won't apologize for declaring that black in any sun kissed shade is beautiful

Black is strong

Black is gorgeous

Black is unique

I love everything about being black from my crown to feet

Wouldn't change anything about my black if I could

It's too bad for you if my blackness is misunderstood

It's kind of hard to explain something that is so exquisitely divine

How we set everything into motion since the beginning of time,

How greatness flows like rivers throughout our
lifelines
The foundation of where humanity was sprung
I will not apologize for my past, my present nor
what's to come
Please move to the left and just let my blackness be
It's too bad if you were seriously expecting an
apology
My blackness is not anything that you and I need to
discuss
Quite frankly, the way I see it, if anyone is owed an
apology it is us

ON THE HORIZON

On the horizon
A drum beats
A warrior chants
Throughout the Horn of Africa
Singing songs that linger on the leaves of
Frankincense trees

Mutilated moans muffled
By tribal cries of consent
Though no blood is yet shed
She is already emotionally hemorrhaging

Innocence spread
As crowds look on
Basking in the glory of what is her womanhood
Now realized by how she sways when she walks
Witchdoctors and dated doctrine deprive her from
the decision
So she lays still
Eyes dilated
Observing "Victor's" misshapen tools of choice
She lays bare
Examined for dissection

He begins
Intense heat,
Her insides on fire as tears cool her face
He
Separates delicate flesh from her body
Drops of her life drip on mud mutilated by surgical
rape

What should be held a sacred place for desire,
Now replaced with pain and embarrassment
Infibulation
Womanhood reduced to a small hole
For piss and mother nature
Now she is deemed chaste
The tribe cries out
Signifying her newly found hack-job purity

No one will ever know her wounds
Keloid scar tissue
Hidden underneath misshapen panties
Scars that run deeper than what was between her legs
Scars that will never heal
Physically disfigured
Emotionally mutilated

THEY JUST CALL IT
SOUTHERN HOSPITALITY

They just call it Southern Hospitality
But we know so much is said with a head nod
They just call it Southern Hospitality because they
Cannot understand that in this land
We nonverbally speak the echoes of generations
You see he does not know me
And I do not know him
Just two random passerby's on the street
That move swiftly to inadvertently toss…a head nod
So much is spoken in that gesture
It says I may not know your destination babygirl but I
certainly can relate to the journey
It says I understand how it is to work two jobs to put
food on the table
It says I understand standing in the middle of the street
praying the #25 comes so you can rest your feet
It says I understand toting one baby on your hip and
another in the stroller
It says I understand fighting the system
It says I understand wondering how you gonna pay
rent and still put gas in the car
It says I understand shakin yo ass for a few sweaty
dollars left in a g-string
It says I understand being the last hired and the first
fired
It says I understand packing ice in your freezer
because you couldn't afford to pay the electricity bill
It says I understand having a momma on crack and
daddy that pimped her out

It says I understand being Black in this whitewashed
world
Nothing needs to be said…just a head nod
Just a head nod
Just a head nod
Just a head nod
And we have reached an understanding
And as we pass, silently in that head nod we root, we
cheer, we encourage them to continue on the journey
You see they…they just call it Southern Hospitality,
but he and me and we…we just call it understanding

GIVE ME MY WONDER BREAD

Give me my Wonder Bread
And I want the entire loaf
I am tired of settling for the crumbs
Because somewhere in life I was taught
That crumbs were enough
That leftovers were sufficient
That a Tupperware existence was okay
That a back burner lifestyle was acceptable
That Saran Wrap dreams could sustain me
But today I've learned that aluminum foil ambitions
is not enough
So give me my Wonder Bread
The flaky, crusty ends and everything in between
Don't throw anything anyway
I want it all
Not just for me but for every woman that came before
me
No longer will I be content with the scraps
Give me my ancestor's injera
Give me grandmother's saltwater cornbread
And my mother's flaky biscuits
Give me my croissants, my sweet Hawaiian rolls, my
baguettes
My soul is done living a carb-free existence
Give me my Wonder Bread
I will not settle for anything less
Because settling is no longer an option
I have learned that it is I, not anyone else, that teaches
people how to treat me
I have taught people
That crumbs were enough

That being last was fine
That being overlooked was acceptable
That others deserved the promotion
That their needs were greater than mine
I sat nibbling at the crumbs
Foolishly fighting others that were starving and not
them that hold the loaf
Because I was complacent with the taste of mere
morsels
That will never sustain me
So give me my Wonder Bread
Coat it in hand churned butter
Sweet honey from the rock
Deep, black cane molasses
Rich, Vermont maple syrup
Homemade grape preserves
And anything that is good, savory, tasty, sweet,
delicious
Because my soul is famished
My being is malnourished
And I have learned that crumbs will never be enough
to satiate this hunger
So give me my Wonder Bread

LOVE & REVOLUTION

She existed outside of herself
Wanted her life to stand for something more
Justice Righteousness Freedom flowed through her
veins
Some called her a revolutionary-A modern day
Angela Davis fighting for equality
Language was the loom on which she weaved
Swahili & Yoruba dialect
To create tapestries of understanding

In the morning before the dawn she inhaled nicotine
While chastising her will for submitting to her
addiction
Addiction equaled weakness
In her life weakness was an obstacle that could
impede the progress of liberty

She kept herself isolated
Knowing that emotional ties
Made it hard to accept the fact
That perhaps one day she would be martyred for her
stance

Only two were able to penetrate her fortress
One slept silently in his room never knowing that she
was laying the foundation for his future
To him...she was just mommy

The other...knew her intimately
Crept behind her as she welcomed the new dawn

Caressed the small of her back
Kissed her midnight skin
Ran his fingers through hair scented with Olive and
Jojoba oil
At that moment, her guard was down
The white flag of surrender rose
She was overcome with lust, passion, need
He planted his lips on the crux of her neck
While his fingers hardened by life massaged her
shoulders
Easing the pain that being a revolutionary caused
He took the hurt away-even the hurt that he had
caused years ago
Kissed down the spine of her back
Ran his tongue along her frustrations
Of loving a man whose love was once contained in a
cell
He was here now, it was okay, she could let go
If only for a moment
But it was this moment
Where instead of screaming no justice no peace
She moaned his name softly
Yet loud enough for him to know that she needed
more
He understood that even as strong as she was
Sometimes, she needed to allow herself to be weak
He offered her that
And she accepted it unapologetically
As her legs spread
Inviting him in
Passion in her eyes demanded it rough, hard, fast,
intense

But beyond the surface he knew that was not what
she needed
So he made love to her slowly
Ran his tongue over hardened nipples
His manly hands wrapped around her small frame
Encasing them in desire
He entered her as she wrapped her legs around him
He pushed deeper
Beyond the hurt, beyond the pain, beyond the past,
beyond the sentence,
beyond the cell block, beyond the justice, beyond the
liberty, beyond the righteousness,
beyond...beyond...beyond...it all
And in that moment
It was....
Just a Nubian God and a Nubian Goddess
Just a Black man and Black woman
Making love passionately, intimately, recklessly
With no thoughts of revolution between them...

COLOR ME

COLOR ME... COLOR ME... COLOR ME
IN SHADES... IN SHADES ...IN SHADES
OF EBONY SILK
DIPPED IN MAHOGANY MILK
COVER MY LIPS WITH OAK BRONZE
AND DIP MY ARMS
WITH STRENGTH
LIKE MY SISTERS THAT TOILED IN FIELDS
OF IVORY
COLOR ME... COLOR ME... COLOR ME
LIKE KUNTA OR TOBY
WITH CRUCIFIED, CRISSCROSSED SCARS ON
BACKS OF RED
LIKE SHADES OF MY HEART
SOULS WEEP BUT NOT DEAD
YET
BLOOD RED, LIKE FAMILIES TORN APART
COLOR ME... COLOR ME... COLOR ME
IN SHADES... IN SHADES... IN SHADES
OF BLACK
WHERE OUR PEOPLE SUFFER BUT NEVER LACK
BECAUSE WE PACKED ON OUR BACKS THE
RYTHM OF
SWING LOW SWEET CHARIOT
COMING FORTH TO CARRY ME HOME
COLOR ME...COLOR ME...COLOR ME
UNTIL I FIND THE PLACE WHERE I BELONG
COLOR ME
IN SHADES OF MY HISTORY
UNTIL ALL OF ME
IS NOTHING BUT A RAINBOW
FOR MY SEED
TO SEE
COLOR ME...COLOR ME...COLOR ME...

WE ARE NOT FINISHED

We are not finished
We have just begun
Don't be fooled for one minute
Barack is only one

How can WE be finished
When liquor stores are on the same blocks as our schools?
How can WE be finished
When crack houses have zip codes in our neighborhoods?
How can WE be finished
When we still make JUST enough money to be broke?
How can WE be finished
When we STILL struggling to find a pot and a window?
How can WE be finished
When we on Maury trying to find out WHO THE BABY DADDY
How can WE be finished
When 56 percent of our kids are raised in single parent homes?
How can WE be finished
When it's STILL a crime to be driving while Black?
How can WE be finished
When we still the usual suspect on the 5 o'clock news
How can WE be finished
When we conveniently killin one another over the color of a handkerchief bought at the dolla store
No! We are not finished

We are not finished as long as I can walk out the doors of any church in my neighborhood, go to the corner and still get a dime bag
No we are not finished
Not as long as women still feel the only way to make it out is to swing from a pole or prostitute on a corner
Not as long as our sons look up to pimps and pushers like they are project royalty
Not as long as a Black man can be gunned down on the subway by police and the likely excuse is "he was resisting".
No we are not finished
Not as long as our little Black boys can't read but coaches say it's okay cause they can bounce a ball
Not as long as the only future our little Black girls see is to be video vixens
I said
We are not finished
Not as long as we continue to kill each other over a hood that don't belong to us no way
No we are not finished
Not as long as our young Black women continue to be the case study for new HIV cases
No we are finished
Not as long as another Black teenage girl is birthing a baby and she is still a baby herself
No we are not finished
Not as long as a racist comic can run in a national newspaper and we are supposed to shuck and jive and take it as a joke
No we are not finished

Not as long as our young girls only aspire to twerk to misogynistic tunes
No we are not finished

Martin Luther King once said, "And if enough Americans were awakened to the injustice; if they joined together, North and South, rich and poor, Christian and Jew, then perhaps that wall would come tumbling down, and justice would flow like water, and righteousness like a mighty stream.

But I say, I don't want justice to flow like water, I don't want righteousness to flow like a mighty stream
We won't be finished not until
Equality
Liberation
Understanding
Justice
SWEEPS THROUGH THIS COUNTRY LIKE A ROARING TSUANAMI
And purges this society of the seeds of
Indignation
Hatred
Racism
And
Indifference
Only then will I be able to declare that I, We, Us
ARE FREE AT LAST
Until then we continue in this fight
Not fooled, not blind sighted, not hindered
by elections and t-shirts and hats and pins

Not tricked and fooled into believing
that centuries of oppression have been wiped out in
ONE DAY!
Until that day comes we continue on in this journey
KNOWING THAT WE ARE NOT FINISHED!

I AM SUFFERING FROM PTSD

Post-traumatic stress disorder
A disorder that develops after a person is exposed to
one or more traumatic events
Major stress
Terrorism or threats on a person's life
A disorder often seen in those that have been in war
I have concluded that I am suffering from PTSD
Because America is a war zone
And each day that I am in this skin I am suited up for
combat
Every day that I walk out of my door I step onto the
battlefield
I am ill equipped for the armored trucks, automatic
weapons,
Tanks and red dots zoomed in on my chest
This is genocide or maybe you can relate if I call it
"ethnic cleansing"
Perhaps if I put a yellow star on the armband of
injustice you can understand
Whatever way you need me to dress it up
Put pain and heartbreak in pretty pumps
Paint despair with red lips, and give it features and
colors that suit you
Like hues of blond and blue then maybe you will see
I am suffering from **P**ost-**T**raumatic **S**lave **D**isorder
Centuries of oppression, Years of abuse, Families
divided, History devastated
That you want me to somehow white wash from my
consciousness
I am suffering from **P**lacating **T**hose that
Systematically **D**estroy

Africa pillaged, America hijacked
From smallpox blankets to Tuskegee experiments
Your fingerprints leaving remnants of your
destruction
I am suffering from Promises That Seem Depleted
Hope that wavers like tattered bloodstained banners
Faith that is hanging on by a thin thread of belief that
one day things will change
Waging war within myself
Fighting the thing within me that tells me to love my
enemies
Because right now…right now the bitterness of hate
taste so sweet
I am suffering from Police That Shoot Daily
With no warning, with no regard, with no thought,
with no care
All because, "Their presence made me feel
threatened",
"I thought he had weapon", "She was reaching for
something"
"He didn't look like he belonged in this
neighborhood"
"Three of them were together so of course they were
up to no good"
I am suffering from People That Simplify
Devastation
Entire lives reduced to rhetoric from people that pace
through palaces of privilege
That sit in anchor chairs behind desks and give
FAUX News reports
Distorting the truth with sugarcoated lies

That toss out code words like thug with a wink to disguise their deep rooted despise
For me and those that look like me
I am suffering from **P**ools **T**hat **S**till **D**iscriminate
Because in America swimming while black is now a crime…just add that one to the list along with driving, walking, running, shopping, breathing, just being
I am suffering from judges and prosecutors **P**imping **T**he **S**ystem **D**aily
A system that purports to be about justice yet the only ones left out was just us
Yet we are foolish enough to continue to trust a system whose every existence resides in pimpin' the weak and less fortunate
The scales of justice were never balanced
I am suffering from **P**reachers **T**hat **S**eem **D**ocile
Too afraid to speak out, too fearful to stand up
Too focused on the great by and by to recognize that God said he came so that we may have life and have it more abundantly; not later but now and if not now than when?
Entire movements that changed the course of history took place in the basements of rickshaw churches with weathered sideboards
This is the time for righteous indignation
I need leaders with Queen Vashti blood in their veins
Because perhaps you are in position for such a time as this!
I am suffering from **P**eople **T**hat **S**adly **D**ecide that I should just get over it

Yet want to have a moment of silence and
remembrance for every other tragedy in history but
mine
I am suffering from **P**eople **T**hat **S**till **D**eny that
racism exists
People that believe we live in a post racial world
cause after 43 presidents they finally let one in
That I should be happy because now I get a chance
to sit at the table instead of bus the table
That I should gladly shuck and jive because they
have decided to give me my rights
I am suffering from **P**eople **T**hat **S**electively
Discriminate
Cause they're cool with me
So they don't mean me, they mean "them"
They ain't racist cause they have 4 Black Twitter
followers and 3 ethnic Facebook friends
I am suffering from **PTSD**
Purchasing **T**-shirts **S**ignifying **D**eath
Popularizing **T**he **S**logans of the **D**eceased
Surrounded by **P**eople **T**hat are **S**enselessly **D**ying
Police that **T**hink **S**urrendering is an act of **D**efiance
Painfully **T**hinking Something will be **D**ifferent
Writing **P**oetry **T**hat **S**creams **D**isaster
And I am tired
And I am angry
And the pain that seeps in my veins runs deep
And no matter how loud I scream help me
Sadly, I don't even know if this is something that
you can treat
I am Suffering from PTSD

CHARLESTON, SOUTH CAROLINA

Angry does not even begin to describe the way that I
feel
My emotions are laid out like a seven dollar and
ninety-nine cent buffet
Pissed off
Sad
Discouraged
Pained
Enraged
Hurt
Bewildered
Dumbfounded
Infuriated
Pick one
Pick two
Or load up your plate with the weight of my despair
There is a smorgasbord of emotions for you to
choose from
Top it all off with blind eyes
Lies
Seeds of hate that continue to be planted
A justice system that continues to specialize in
failure
At 39 I have survived lies
Fair-weather friends
Domestic violence
Homeless shelters
The list of my endurance is endless
Yet this is the only situation that made me truly
question God

How is this fair?
How is this right?
How do you expect me to sleep at night?
How do you expect people to survive?
How is the continual massacre of innocence okay?
How do people that pray turn to prey?
I do not have all the answers
Yet in that moment, hours, days of my doubt, I am reminded
That there was a man
That loved unconditionally
That sacrificed daily
That gave of himself with no regard of himself
That stared impending death in the eye and said, "Nevertheless, Thy will be done"
That defiantly said, "No one takes my life but I lay it down and if I lay it down, I have the authority to pick it back up again"
That sat among those that he knew would betray him
That remained silent in the face of accusations
That was a lamb led to the slaughter
That still said, "Father, forgive them for they know not what they do"
Admittedly, I am not there yet but I am trying...
I don't have the answers
Yet I have to believe because I have nothing else to believe
Do not fret because of those who are evil or be envious of those who do wrong;
For like the grass they will soon wither, like green plants they will soon die away.
I have to stand on the word that says,

"If my people, who are called by my name, will humble themselves and pray and seek my face and turn from their wicked ways, then I will hear from heaven, and I will forgive their sin and will heal their land."

When my soul is in turmoil I have to remember that, He makes his sun rise on the evil and on the good, and sends rain on the just and on the unjust.

Believe me, I am struggling and I am hurting

So no, I don't know the right thing to say

But every day I have to believe that one day vengeance will truly be his…

WAILS ON THE WILLOWS...

Darkness yields its hold giving way to dawn
The sun rest just beneath the horizon
We wait...
Anticipating a new day that never seems to come
The air does not shift
Instability lingers like dew on grass blades
Still we wait...
We stand at a crossroads
Race now intersects with gender
Wondering which cross Justice will choose to bear?
Front lines fueled by the resounding chants of names
once unknown now etched into history
Yet, somehow *their* names are lost among the
propaganda
They have no slogans
Cardboard signs hold no names
Final words lost in the shuffle of no justice, no
peace...
In death, they find no justice, no peace
In the stillness of the new day
We wait...
Blood pleads from just beneath the surface of
Mother Earth
Yearning to be heard
Echoes that seem like mere whispers
Remain muted no longer
Shantel Davis
Rekia Boyd
Sandra Bland
Tyisha Miller
Yvette Smith

Shereese Francis
Aiyana Jones
Natasha McKenna
Mothers
Daughters
Sisters
Women
Black…Women…the bitter sharpness of a double-edged sword
Race and gender, where rock and hard place often collide
We declare that you will be silenced no more
No longer invisible
We hear you
We are the voices of ancestors, of generations
We are the wombs that birthed nations
We are the voices of old Negro spirituals
We are backs that bore the lashes of injustice
We are shoulders that carried the weight of suffering
We are strength personified
So no longer do we wait…
Today amidst the new dawn
We speak
We shout
We scream
We yell
Vowing that the blood that wails, wrestling through the willows will be heard…

#HASHTAG

A hashtag is a type of label used on social networks which makes it easier for users to find messages with a specific theme or content.

#Hashtag
Growing up
everyone I knew
wanted to be
famous
Hollywood bound
The big screen

Faces donning the cover of A-list magazines
Names flashing in neon lights
Top billing on Broadway billboards
Stars on the Walk of Fame
Names engraved in sidewalks
Flashes from cameras as the paparazzi longs to catch just a glimpse
Of us in our magnificence
All we wanted to do…was make it
Hashtag
Million dollar deals
Hollywood homes in the hills
Taking trips to Madrid
Just because we wanted to get away for the weekend
Sipping Dom Perignon on yachts
Gucci handbags
Clothes made by the finest designers and
Shoes made by names we can't even pronounce

But we own them
Stunting in our stilettos
Makeup flawless, beat to the Gawds
Lookin' like we woke up like this must be hard
#Hashtag
Now fame is so much easier to come by
Enough hits on a YouTube video
And you are famous
Enough likes and you make the Huffington Post
All we need is for one thing to go viral
Enough tears, enough bullet wounds, enough blood shed and
CNN will take notice
MSN will put every Facebook picture you ever took on its homepage
Just as long as you look like the usual suspect
You are now a trending topic
You have become the latest hashtag
Your name will be first in a google search
Your death will be forever memorialized on T shirts
#Trayon Martin
Eric Garner
Sandra Bland
Tamir Rice
#Mike Brown
Oscar Grant
Aiyana Jones
Reykia Boyd
#Kendric McDade
Kimani Gray
John Crawford
Sean Bell

Shantel Davis
Yvette Smith
Paparazzi pics are now autopsy photos
And hits are now endured by police sticks
The flash of lights are now red and blues
Famous quotes are last words whispered by those dying
Million dollar deals are now police misconduct payouts
Walk of Fame dreams are now roadside memorials
Stars in sidewalks are now bodies in blood stained streets
Obscure names are now known…worldwide
Not because of their talent
But as those that died
Simply for being black the wrong time
Hashtags are now digital toe tags
Marking the names of the deceased
And my childhood dreams of being famous
Have ceased
The curtain has been called
Yet please ladies and gentlemen hold your applause
As we wait for the encore
Of the next young black person
That longs to be famous…

Hannah L. Drake

KEEPER

Keep him
Protect him
Love him
Watch over him
Care for him
Chestnut eyes look similar
Underneath black lashes
Skin once flawlessly chocolate
Rich with melanin, veins flowing with future
Body once strong now scarred and marred with
through and through wounds
Too young
Too soon
His name barely makes a headline
Quick blurbs at 5 o' clock news
Another black male dead
The phrase so common
Yet still it echoes in my mind
Reverberating
Not again
When will this end?
When did the value of a life become so cheap?
Murder is senseless
Over shoes, over drugs, over streets we don't own
And I'm angry
Because people are standing on the front lines
Fighting a war that's being waged against black men
And you…you
Did this?
With no thought of the ramifications
Your senseless act of misguided manhood

Would heap on the masses screaming
Black Lives Matter
To who?
Not you.
How can I defend a black life to them
When a black life didn't matter to another black man
And what you just did
Set an entire movement back again
Allows them to point fingers and say, "see."
Your actions help justify in their minds injustice.
Just how do you want me to defend that?
I'm tired
Of trying to get you to see the potential and power that
you possess
Trying to wake you from your slumber
Yet you continue to hit the snooze button
And count sheep determined to stay asleep
And the alarm is sounding
Yet you don't hear it
You are blinded
When will you wake up and see?
Life is bigger than the moment you pull that trigger
There is no coming back from that road
His life mattered
You have robbed a mother
You have stolen something from our community
You have hijacked a movement with your senseless
act of violence
Shame on you!
Look at him
His eyes
His hair

His skin
He was Africa
He was scars on whipped backs
He was a civil rights movement
He was the pride in our hearts seeing the first black
president
He was a black man
And his life mattered
Black lives do matter
But they must first matter to us
Am I my brother's keeper?
Yes. I AM!

THE PLANE IS ON FIRE

A thin curtain is all that separates
Us from Them
They revel in the delight of First Class
Content
Enjoying ample leg room and plush pillows
Seats reclined
Sipping chilled champagne
Dining on penne with pesto and spring salad
Oblivious to those that walk the aisle between them
They do not make eye contact
If they do not look, they cannot see
As we walk by, carry-on bag in hand
We understand that we are not them
We ride in Coach
Seats pressed too tightly together
Reclining, although an option,
We reject because we understand
The space is simply too tight
We do not want to inconvenience others for our
comfort
We understand the struggle
Stewardess comes by and we are
Content with 12 ounce cans of soda only poured half
way in plastic cups
And dry honey roasted peanuts
We sip our drink slowly
Swallowing down peanuts packed years ago
Knowing we will get off soon
We will reach our destination
Yet they
In First Class

Will be the
First off
They were the first on
And when the plane lands
We will wait
For them.
Privileged
High Class
First Class
They are not us
And we are not them
Perhaps it is simple economics that keep us divided
Even more than that thin curtain
Yet
One thing remains the same
No matter the class…
"Ladies and gentlemen, welcome aboard Flight 2125 with non-stop service to Chicago. Please turn your attention to the flight attendant nearest you for our safety demonstration. Please follow along with the safety card located in the seat pocket in front of you
In case there is a loss in cabin pressure, yellow oxygen masks will deploy from the ceiling compartment located above you. To secure, pull the mask towards you, secure the elastic strap to your head, and fasten it so it covers your mouth and nose. Breathe normally. Even if the bag does not inflate, please keep in mind that oxygen is flowing. Please make sure to secure your own mask before assisting others.

Thank you for your attention, and we wish you a good flight."

No matter the class
No matter the bank account
No matter the position
If the plane should find itself in distress
If the plane should catch on fire
The ENTIRE PLANE IS ON FIRE
The fire will not stop
At first class
And right now…right now
THE PLANE IS ON FIRE
And it's a small fire
Just starting to engulf Coach
It is us now
But soon…Soon it will be you
Because injustice is like smoke
It has a way of
Seeping through corners
Creeping through zip codes
Finding a way to your front door
Chickens do come home to roost
Believe this truth
If we burn…EVERYONE BURNS!
This is bigger than us
It is bigger than race
This is bigger than gender
This is bigger than any label that can be placed on us
The world will soon boil down to the have and the
have nots
You have been lulled asleep the great American
lullaby believing that you are in a group with the
haves
You are not

If you are poor you are in coach
If you are gay you are in coach
If you are disabled you are in coach
If you are elderly you are in coach
If you are not one of them you are in coach
Coach has nothing to do with your race
But will soon have everything to do with power.
Your status will not save you
Your 401K does not make you immune
The plane is on fire
Flames all around us
Engulfing us
In order to save you
You must save us
And in order to save us
We must save you
We are in this together
Working towards a bigger goal
Justice for one is not enough
Justice for all is the only way to extinguish the
flames
The plane is on fire
And if we burn…you burn…
Thank you for flying with us today…

HANNAH L. DRAKE

Hannah Drake offers an inspirational message that has been heard in various arenas and has performed her poetry at the Legendary Showtime at the Apollo. She is frequently asked to speak throughout the country, offering an inspiring, poetic message of hope and deliverance believing that her words will ultimately be used for true transformation. In 2014 she joined Roots and Wings, a dynamic group of artists that seek to bring social change within their community. In 2015 Hannah Drake, along with the members of Roots and Wings were able to perform their written play, The West End Poetry Opera, at the Kentucky Center for the Performing Arts. In addition, Hannah Drake was a guest poet at the Festival of Faiths offering poetry on social justice, believing that communication is truly the beginning of change. Her powerful, honest delivery has garnered her the nickname, "Brimstone".

Hannah is the author of several works of poetry, Hannah's Plea-Poetry for the Soul, Anticipation, Life Lived In Color, In Spite of My Chains and So Many Things I Want to Tell You-Life Lessons for the Journey. Her debut novel Views from the Back Pew was received with stellar reviews and was performed on stage to a sold out audience. Her follow up novel, Fragile Destiny has been hailed as life changing.

Hannah Drake is currently working on her new publishing company Drake Publishing which desires to give a voice to all writers that have a message as well as several novels in the works.

I am honored, blessed and humbled that I have been given this opportunity. My life has taken me on a series of journeys, paths I never thought that I would walk and roads I never should have traveled but in all pain, there is purpose. The Bible says all things work together for the good of those who love Him and are called according to His purpose-this is my purpose and this is good.

There are many layers to who I am as a person and as an author. All of it is reflected within the pages of my books. I do not make any apologies for writing it the way I feel it, the way I see it, the way I experience it. This is simply my voice!

Keep reading and I'll keep writing.

OTHER BOOKS BY HANNAH DRAKE

Novels
- Views from the Back Pew
- Fragile Destiny

Poetry Collections
- Hannah's Plea
- In Spite of My Chains
- Life Lived In Color
- Anticipation

Self Help
- So Many Things I Want To Tell You

All books available at www.hannahldrake.com

CONTACT INFORMATION

- hld@hannahldrake.com
- Facebook: hannah.drake628
- Twitter: hannahdrake628

Made in the USA
Columbia, SC
29 May 2021

38698819R10065